I0749011

(*analog*) CRUISING

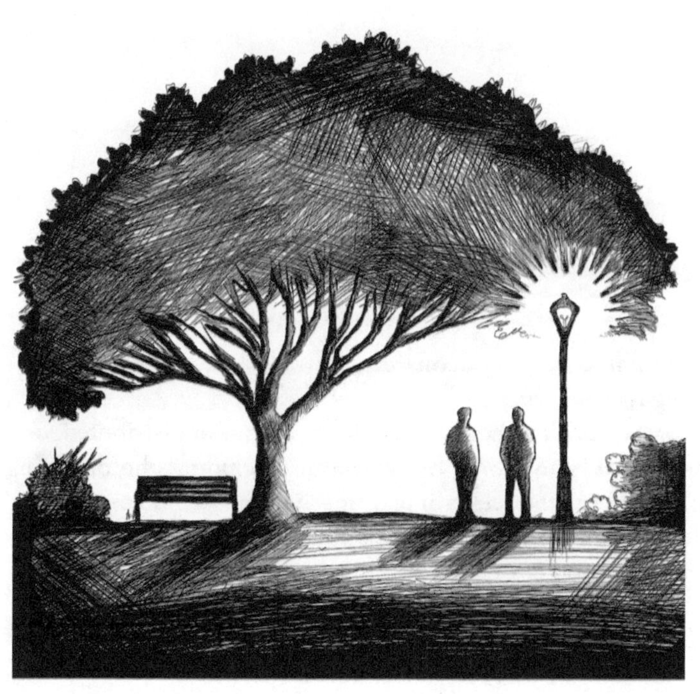

Second Edition 2024
ISBN: 979-8-9895418-5-0

Layout design by L. Herrera and J. R. Sperber
Cover design by J.R. Sperber, L. Herrera and B. LaBauve
Illustrations by L. Herrera
Editing by A. Gonsher and J. R. Sperber,
Printed in The United States of America by Blurb
3325 S 116th St, Tukwila, WA 98168

www.leoherrera.com

PROLOGUE

BATHHOUSE
STREET
NATURE
DARKROOM
ARCADE
SEX CLUB
BAR

APPS (EPILOGUE)

Berlin, 2022

I can't sleep and my spot is too hot to write in. What better place to beat a heatwave and writer's block than a notorious darkroom?

I started writing this guide in Berlin because its sex spaces have been infamous for over a century. Germany is, after all, the birthplace of the word "homosexual," coined in 1868. Nearly every bar in the gayborhood has a sex area, each with a different pulse. One bar hosts the younger, hip crowd; another brings out the bears, and there's one slick fetish bar with impeccable lighting for men who spend fortunes on leather regalia. There's a quaint dive frequented by Turkish sex workers, another for horny septuagenarians. Most close at sunrise. Those who didn't find what they were looking for – or who pretended they weren't looking – will end up where I am, in the area's only 24-hour bar, nicknamed "the drain of Berlin."

The bar itself is just an excuse for the darkroom.

Its seats are uncomfortable, utilitarian metal benches that are easy to hose down. The bartenders are chill unless they catch you darting to the back without buying a drink; then they bark in German. Men come at all hours to buy a shot, then shoot a load. The darkroom is sparse, with two platforms like little stages, slings hanging from industrial chains dropped in the middle of the room. It's almost pitch-black but for strips of red LED lights.

I'm waiting for my Mpox vaccine to kick in, so I won't be partaking in the action tonight. I'll be back in a week to paint these walls, but for now I'm here to observe. I buy a cheap beer and take a seat. I sink into the dissociation of watching a play. There's a new show here every night.

A handsome boy in a leather harness is bent over the bench next to me, getting railed. He's got a death grip on a bottle of amyl nitrite. For a moment, its sweet cherry odor blocks out the moldy, sweaty sex smells of the room. He's trying to close the cap with lubed hands but he might as well be attempting it in an earthquake. I reach over and close it for him. He looks up and smiles at me. Territorially, the top starts to jackhammer harder until the boy's eyes roll back and he turns away, face down on the sticky bench.

The barback comes in with a flashlight, picking up glasses, maneuvering around the sex, illuminating the two slings. Two thin, older men are swaying on them, leisurely masturbating. Legs up in the air like two skinny, trussed-up Costco chickens, their anuses gape and wink when a new man enters. I stare into their holes in a trance.

I run to the bathroom to jot some notes on my phone and when I get back, the boy getting fucked is replaced by a short blond bearded guy and a tall nerd in glasses. The blond is grinning and the nerd is slack-jawed. "My mate's first time," he says proudly to me in a British accent. "I'm going to get another beer." He winks at me as if he's setting us up and walks away, leaving the nerd stirring his cocktail over and over. He's wearing a polo shirt, his hair parted carefully, his posture rigid. Every kind of Gay comes in here, but he still manages to look painfully out of place. And there's not many rules here, but being on your phone is forbidden. Without any distraction, he's got no choice but to watch the show.

He sits next to me but not too close. "I hope nobody tries to touch me," he mutters with a shaky laugh. I feel bad for him. His friend should have eased him into the culture shock. "No one's going to touch you if you don't want it," I say gently. "And if they do, you just do this." I take my hand and gently tap-tap on his arm, as if I'm trying to move him out of the way. "The international symbol of darkroom rejection." He nods, takes a big swig and watches, riveted and horrified. A short man walks in, lays on the platform in front of us, pulls down his pants and tighty-whities and gets on all fours. A beat later, a man walks from across the room, pulls down his own pants and tighty-whities, and mounts him without saying a word. They both stare at us, then roll their heads back in pleasure. It's too much for the boy.

"Wow," he exhales. "Well, it was nice to meet you," he says, shaking his head and walking out. I sit for a while longer, finishing my beer. The top comes in a volcanic, theatrical orgasm. "Good for her," I think. The top leaves. The bottom's legs are shaking as he fumbles with his pants. The top returns and hands him paper towels and a beer. Men are capable of such tenderness when there's no fight for sex.

Curtain call. I get up and leave into a night which is finally cooling.

When people say they go to the beach to think, I imagine this is what they mean. These spaces are calming to me. Sometimes it feels we value our sex spaces as we do coral reefs: only when we're on vacation, or when they bleach and die.

I've been cruising these spaces for two decades. I can count on one hand the times I've used an app for sex. So when the parties are over, when the bars close, when my friends head home to fuck their twins or ramble over a plate of powders or swipe and swipe and swipe until the sun comes up, I travel here. To the dank walls of sex theaters in Manhattan and Mexico City. To the glory holes of San Francisco. To the parks in Brooklyn and Berlin. The bathhouses in DC and Chicago. The piers and beaches of Provincetown, Fire Island and Pensacola. The 24-hour bars in New Orleans. The forests of Tennessee, Pennsylvania and Alabama. The sex tents in Black Rock City.

This manual is the lessons I've learned. Some were came through instinct, others through elders. Cruising spaces are porous and versatile—they borrow from one another. Some of these tips may apply to all kinds of cruising, while others are site-specific. The most important thing to remember is that analog cruising is built on a tight honor system of manners. Every space has a level of *implied consent* that depends on this etiquette, given through eye contact and non-verbal cues. We are *all* responsible for the respect of implied consent, even if we don't want to fuck each other.

Cruising is an imperfect art, but most of this becomes common sense and second nature with practice. Cruising spots exist because of oral histories like this. By sharing where these spaces are and how to be, we breathe life into them. Our instincts preserve their purpose, and this etiquette has been passed down since before Queer words were written.

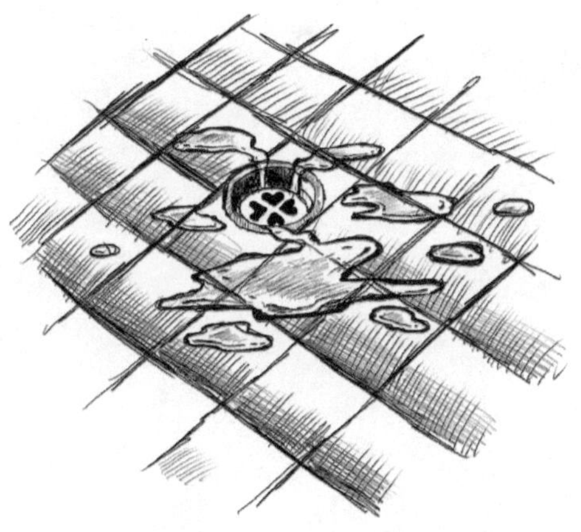

bathhouse

San Francisco, 2004

The first time I saw myself as a "man" was in a bathhouse. It happened in the showers of Eros in 2004. Eros had the best shower heads in all of San Francisco. The pressure on those babies could take the knots off your back. On frigid summer nights, I'd book it to the Castro. I had just moved to the Bay Area from Phoenix, where Gay spaces were rare and tucked away. Eros had a proud, bright awning that let *everyone* know what you were walking into. It was also across from the Safeway from *Tales of the City*. I felt so cosmopolitan. A sweet, cocky bear worked the counter and always had a smirk that made me blush. They were the proud editor of *Cubby*, an FtM porn zine piled at the entrance next to the fag rags.

Eros was cozy. It had a carpeted locker room, a small but crucial steam room, an upstairs playroom with leather beds, and TVs that showed porn shot in the very same bathhouse. It was spotless, but the disinfectant couldn't hide the faint mildew of the carpet. Even if the place was empty, it was worth the price to shower until my fingers pruned, until that June fog melted away. I was scrawny and the cold ocean air got in my bones.

It was a tiny moment. Late at night Eros could feel supernatural, with a Kubrick silence. I was never scared of its ghosts though.

I was alone in the showers after the bars closed. As I walked out, a man charged towards me, arms stretched, posed for an ambush. His body was lithe and alert, stoic and simian. It took an entire second to realize it was a full-length mirror behind the plume of steam. I'd never seen myself hold my body like this. In the outside world, I hunched over and shrunk in front of other boys. I was so self-conscious that I couldn't grow muscle or hair. When I was in here, I carried myself differently. I felt relaxed, patient, *grown*. That night, I finally understood the confidence of the bear at the front. This was the confidence of safety.

Technically, Eros wasn't a bathhouse – those were still banned. They'd been shuttered in San Francisco since 1984. For legal purposes, Eros was a "sauna." A "bathhouse" was defined as having rooms with locks. During the AIDS crisis, health departments didn't trust men to practice safe sex. Locks were prohibited so staff could make sure condoms were being used, usually by going into rooms with a flashlight. The flashlights eventually went away, but the rule over the locks would not be challenged in San Francisco until 2020. Like so many other bathhouses, Eros closed during COVID-19. It will always be one of the places I transitioned from boyhood to adult. I don't remember if I had sex that night, but my reflection is seared in my mind. It would take me years to understand that it was not some secret, extra version of myself, but the *real* one. Gay men love nothing more than seeing ourselves for the first time.

Pick the right time for you. It's okay to be nervous. A place where you have to be naked and "perform" can be intimidating. If you're introverted, go when it's chill to familiarize yourself. If you're a deep end kind of Queer, pick a holiday like Pride. Each day and time of the week has its own vibe. For example, weekday afternoons and early evenings are usually for an older crowd relaxing after work. Sundays are for a mix of folks self-caring before the week or partiers recovering from the weekend. Long holiday weekends are great to meet out-of-towners. Really, really late at night or early mornings on weekends can be the tweaker witching hour. Check on early bird specials, age discounts or two-for-one days. Some even have BBQs! During a long layover in Fort Lauderdale, I got a room at a bathhouse that was a third of the price of a hotel, and tanned daddies served fried chicken by the pool.

Checking into a bathhouse. Places may charge a single cover or a cover plus a membership fee, generally $20-50. You'll get a key or lock for your locker, or a digital wristband. They may store your ID, phone, and valuables at the front. Private rooms can be first come, first served or paid by the hour. Some may give or rent flip-flops and towels. Other places may allow you to bring your own and save you some coins, a great reason to throw a pair in your luggage when you travel. If they sell beverages or food, you generally pay on your way out.

Bring a small bag or fanny pack. You'll most likely be in only a towel, so carry your sex gear like lube and poppers (if the place allows them) in a small, light bag that can get wet. In a pinch, I cut off the elastic part of a sock to use as an armband to keep poppers and lube on me. Unless the front cashier feels especially sketchy and there are no lockers, it's usually a bad idea to carry a phone and valuables.

It's okay to bring a friend. Bathhouses are for socializing as much as sex. Bring a buddy to catch up in the steam room or hot tub, and explore the amenities together.

Keep the volume at a library decibel. If an orgy breaks out in the steam room, maybe keep your opinions on your pop diva's new single to yourself for a minute.

Don't be real fucked up. This goes for all cruising. A swig of liquid courage is one thing, but a drunken blackout or stumbling on G like you're going to break your skull on a tile or tree stump is not hot. Being a coked-out chatterbox or going into a K-hole obliterates the vibes for everyone and can get you seriously hurt. The heat of a steam room or hot tub drops your blood pressure and multiplies the effects of downers like G, K, and booze, and can also increase the dangers of mixing erectile medications and poppers. Hydrate more than you think you need. A heat-resistant metal water bottle is great for prolonged sessions in a steam room or hot tub.

Private rooms may invite heavy drug use, so really

messed up folks can unfortunately be part of the cruising experience, especially in a bathhouse. During International Mr. Leather Weekend in Chicago's biggest bathhouse, I saw a queen who hadn't slept or eaten for three days and it was… not pretty. Avoid being that person and be very careful taking drinks or drugs from strangers.

Implied consent. In cruising spaces, touch is often part of the language of consent. The intimacy of the touch varies depending on the person, moment, and physical space you're in. It typically requires an invitation, usually through eye contact. The invitation can also come in the form of a caress, either on your own body or the other person's—a tug of your crotch, their arm, or the small of their back. These caressing cues build on themselves, leading toward more intimacy.

Every cruising space has a slightly different system of implied consent. In a bathhouse, touching someone in the common areas like a locker room, hot tub and sauna usually requires more initial verbal signs (a simple "hi" is good). Steam rooms, sex mazes and private rooms lean toward the non-verbal. You may make eye contact and play with yourself as your first move. Eye contact is crucial to gauge interest.

If someone is in a room or booth and their door is open, the invitation will be mostly non-verbal.

Stand at the doorway for a moment and hold eye contact. Wait for their invitation or rejection: a soft nod for a yes or a light head-shake for a no. You may both touch or stroke yourselves, and if they hold eye contact and keep going, that may also be an invite. Or they may just flip over for you to get to work.

Rejection. If someone reaches out to touch you and you are not interested, tapping their arm away is standard cruising etiquette. It should be firm but gentle, as if you're moving a dog off the couch. A polite "no thank you" should also suffice. The goal is *always* for *everyone* to feel respected and welcome.

Any cruising area or crowd that doesn't make elders and Trans folks feel welcome isn't worth the lot it stands on. Note: "Being welcome" doesn't necessarily mean getting laid—it means being safe from harassment and able to use all the facilities in peace.

Do not take rejection as a reflection on you. This goes for all cruising areas. If you get a no, just nod courteously and leave their space. You don't know what they're looking for. They may just be a voyeur or exhibitionist or biding their time. It may also mean "not right this minute," and you may connect later.

Madonna once sang, "Rejection is the greatest aphrodisiac." I've always disagreed. I was never turned on by "the chase" or playing hard to get. Games are for kids. But it's telling that "How do I reject or deal with rejection?" is the most common question about analog cruising. A crucial lesson we learn face-to-face is accepting or giving a no with courtesy and empathy. This gets lost in digital cruising, where we can just insult, block, or ghost. It's tempting to romanticize rejection as "nicer" before the apps. It sucks no matter where we are. Dealing with it in person strengthens our emotional immune system and helps us leave scarcity mindsets toward affection and pleasure. A proper rejection may even lead to friendships.

Prince Charming Syndrome. Most cruising spaces are about patience, but don't waste time waiting for the "ideal lover." Berlin's most infamous sex dungeon allows people in for only the first hours of the evening. This is meant to prevent Prince Charming Syndrome, when we spend all of our time waiting for the perfect man and refuse to interact with who is already there. While the club could make ten times more money without this policy, its success and infamy depend on its consistency.

Prince Charming may be an orgasm and not a person. Experiment and try new archetypes. As the drag queen Meatball says, "You're at the buffet, don't just wait around for the crab legs!" It was in a bathhouse that I discovered I was a chubby chaser. A Rubenesque man, surprised at my lust, asked me if I was "parTying or just a wild child." If we'd been out at a bar, it would probably not have occurred to us to go home together. We were both happy for my discovery that Tuesday afternoon.

Value these spaces even if you don't go. Bathhouses have been havens from violence and the cops for generations. They were invaluable for community outreach on AIDS (which made their closures all the more tragic). They've educated us on safe sex, rang the alarm on meningitis, syphilis, and Mpox outbreaks, even administered the vaccines! They foster community outside of the bars and can even be places for art.

My very first photo show was at Eros. It was the only space which would exhibit my porn images, displaying them in the lobby. I watched all my friends come in for their first time for the opening reception. As they curiously scoped out the place I had spent so much time in, I felt like I was welcoming them into my own living room. I understood why so many before me had considered it a home.

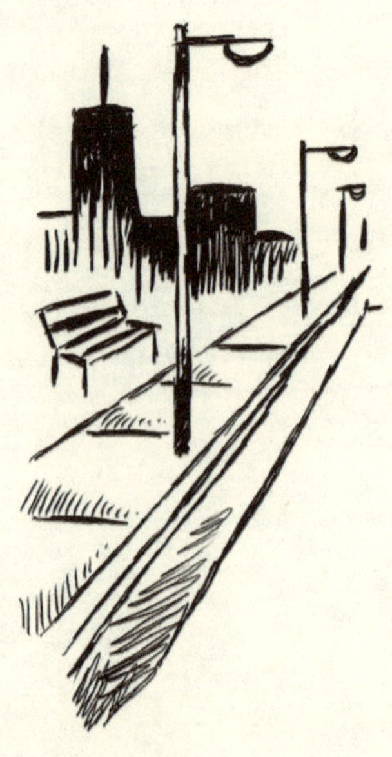

street

Brooklyn, 2012

It was just one of those nights. Everyone I hit on was not interested, and I kept shooting blanks at the bar. After enough rejection, I packed it up and headed home. I got off the subway grumpy and horny. I was a block from my house when I saw a handsome stranger walking toward me. He was staring intently at his phone. He looked up a few feet away from me, and we locked eyes as we passed. I kept walking, and after a few beats, I turned around. He turned around too. I was feeling gun shy from the evening, so I turned away, walked a few more feet, then turned back one more time. He had stopped and was still looking. I walked over.

"Where are you going?" I asked.

"I'm looking for this bar to meet my friend, but I'm turned around." He flashed the map on his phone.

"Let me see." I moved closer to look at his screen. He smelled like salt and cologne.

"Well, that bar is that way..." I pointed back toward the subway. A pause filled the entire block. "But my house is that way." I smirked. So did he.

"Let's go."

A classic cruise depends on a **three-point system:**

1. Lock eyes as you pass.

2. Look back. If they look back, stop.

3. If they stop too, walk toward them.

That's it. In explicit cruising areas like parks, non-verbal communication will be enough. You may tilt your head toward the direction you want to go or grab your crotch to indicate the invitation. On a public street, it requires a little more finesse and an icebreaker. "Where are you going?" is usually sufficient. Why else would you ask a stranger unless you wanted to go with them? If a meetup is not possible that moment, take their number or social media info and say, "I'll find you later."

Walking away without looking back is *way* hotter.

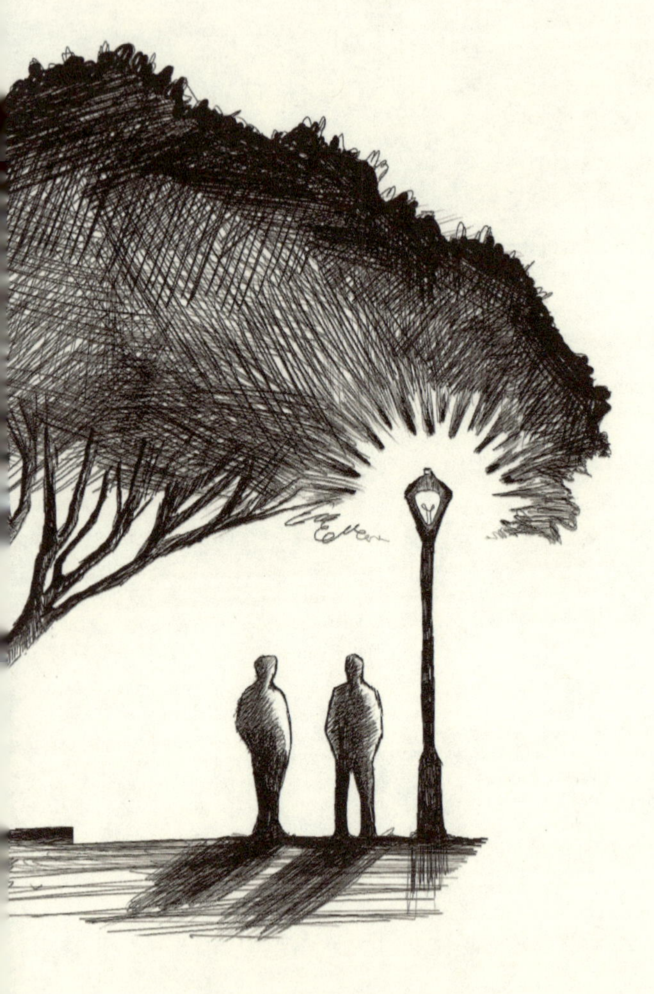

nature

Berlin, 2012

It was dark and I was lost. The park was larger than I could have imagined. My map wasn't loading and my phone was dying. There was no sign of the soldier.

I passed a lake, a restaurant, a beer garden and an open-air cinema. I was not expecting this much life so late into the evening. In America, most parks close at night, swallowed up by their city's shadows. I'd never cruised a park before, but I had been to darkrooms and bathhouses. It couldn't be *that* different, right?

There he was: The *Spanienkämpfer*, sword to the sky. A memorial statue from 1968, honoring the fallen German communist fighters in the Spanish Civil War. There was nothing erotic about him. He was boxy, anatomically incorrect and hunched over.

This was the spot my Berliner friends told me to

look for but there was nobody around. I couldn't just Google it and everyone was at a 72-hour ketamine rave that didn't allow phones. Had I missed it? This couldn't be it. It was just a lawn that opened right into the street. There was nobody to ask for directions even if I had spoken German. I heard the cackling of women far away.

I took a deep breath. I closed my eyes, then opened them to the dark.

OK bitch, think... This park is old as fuck. How did the men before me do it? Horny guys during the war... they had no phones, they couldn't go around asking people where to suck dick in fucking Nazi Germany. Where do we go? Away from the street. Away from the lawn. Away from laughing straight people. Into the dark. Into the quiet. Into a place where we can see out but they can't see in.

The summer sun never fully sets in Berlin and the parks are never truly dark. A milky light illuminates them like a full moon out of frame. It's a vampiric sight, where the trees look like tricks and tricks look like trees. The opening materialized out of the gnarled trees, which craned their neck to a tiny path out of a fairytale.

Maybe a shortcut to the other side of the park, to find the subway and go home, I negotiated with myself, knowing damn well my dick might be making terrible choices.

The tree canopy was dead. Either this wasn't the place or I had missed the wild park orgy. It was better when I didn't know what this was going to be. I checked my phone's dying screen and useless map one more time.

Out of the corner of my eye, I saw an orange firefly. Then another, and another—hovering. It was the glow of cigarettes. I felt my ears flush, and my heart started to pound. Figures had been sitting and standing, watching me. *I'm already inside.* My chest tightened. The air smelled faintly of some kind of berry, mixed with the waft of cigarettes, dirt, and beer. The *ticktickti ck* of a bicycle echoed nearby.

A tall man was standing a few feet away from me. I walked up to him and he didn't walk away. I got close enough to kiss him. He didn't back away but he turned his face to the side. *No kissing.* He had strong features, a crew cut, a thick, fit body in a polo shirt and white jeans. He smelled like soap but not cologne. He had showered not too long ago. He tugged at his dick over his jeans. *The invitation.*

I reached out and touched it. It was hard, like calcium. He touched me only once, to take my entire head in one huge palm and gently, but firmly, push it down.

Brooklyn, 2015

I wasn't in a hurry to get home. The huge fight I just had with my boyfriend was going to keep me up all night. I couldn't imagine being this angry in a packed subway, so I decided to stomp through Prospect Park even though it was an hour after it closed.

Prospect Park has more majesty than Central Park. Makes sense, since it was the sequel from the folks who designed Manhattan's crown jewel. Instead of a rectangular grid, Prospect has nooks and meadows and no city roads interrupt it.

During the day, families fly kites in wide lawns where it's easy to monitor children—those little magicians who teleport and disappear. It's open for the safety of women, who can laugh over a bottle of rosé without fear of getting dragged behind a bush and assaulted. Police can move in with ostentatious displays of safety and authority, handing out tickets for drinking the rosé. At night, those open spaces are lit like a high school football field—Friday night lights for a crowd who isn't even allowed here after midnight. Heterosexuality requires its own terrain.

I had a huge bag of weed on me, my laptop, and my toiletries—the fight was pretty bad. I was more scared of a bored cop looking to fill a ticket quota than getting mugged, so I took the dark trail in the general direction of my apartment. Once the anger cooled, it didn't take long for me to regret that decision.

Why was I wandering around a Brooklyn park in the middle of the night with all my belongings? Maybe part of me wanted to get hurt to spite my boyfriend. I picked up the pace, walking toward a park lamp. When I got to it, I heard a branch break very close by.

"Hey." A soft, low voice.

Shit, here we go.

"Do you know where Bedford Avenue is?"

A mugging usually starts with a question. "What time is it?" "Can I borrow your phone?" My body stiffened, ready to run or start swinging.

I turned around and saw a thin boy in his early 20s. The lamp bathed his skin in a sulfur glow. I locked eyes with him and I caught the delicate drop of his eyelashes. Unmistakable softness.

The fight had made me bold and reckless. "I think you know where Bedford Avenue is." I walked toward him. He grinned in three different ways. My dick got hard so fast I could have passed out.

I touched his waist and he melted. I kissed him. His wet mouth tasted like a cherry Jolly Rancher. I pressed my erection against his and walked him backwards, away from the light. We moved in unison toward the tree in an impressive tango. He turned his face toward the bark. I yanked his basketball shorts down and he spread his legs. I took a glob of cherry spit and in a few gentle half-thrusts, I was inside him.

I was delirious at my luck, convinced this was a

cosmic validation for the fight—the universe taking my side and rewarding me for always being right. It wasn’t. I had simply walked into the Vale of Cashmere, a cruising spot for Black and Latino men.

The Vale of Cashmere is a secluded, petite valley created when a glacier melted underground and collapsed the soil, leaving a divot surrounded by steep walls of earth. It’s private and cozy, perfect for cruising. Because of a series of events 17,000 years ago, men gather here to shoot their semen into the soil.

The area I was at used to be a children's playground in the 1800s. There was a pool and gardens, parallel bars, swings and a seesaw. Children sailed miniature boats in a Beaux-Arts fountain. It had lily pads so big, a little girl could float on them. A majestic rose garden bloomed. A Brooklyn mayor’s wife had nicknamed the area the “Vale of Cashmere,” inspired by the Thomas Moore poem “Lalla Rookh, an Oriental

Romance":

Who has not heard of the Vale of Cashmere,
With its roses the brightest that earth ever gave,
Its temples and grottos, and fountains as clear
As the love-lighted eyes that hang over the wave?

The poem is about a princess engaged to a prince who falls in love with a poet who, big shock, turns out to be the prince.

The Vale was prohibitively expensive to maintain for such a hidden area. By the 1960s, the ostentatious garden fell into disrepair. The lily pool became overgrown, the fountains ran dry, the rose bushes withered. The men arrived.

Cruising in nature is embedded in Queer history and imagination. It's primal, thrilling, and dangerous, even illegal—not like that's ever stopped us. It rewards patience and teaches gratitude. There is discipline in accepting that you don't know where your orgasm may come from or if you'll get one. It leaves you with two choices: leave or settle. Not "settle" as in lowering your standards, but in the settler sense of being a pioneer, to take over a piece of earth, stake a claim to a lover. To be open to a sex connection you may have missed in "the real world" under the weight of expectations, prejudice, and stigma. Those who see their lovers as a reflection of who they are, who collect them as trophies, don't tend to thrive in nature. Adventurers do.

Cruising is the art of minimal rejection and consent. A nod, the shy stroke of an arm, the electrifying jolt of eye contact—gestures that predate language. To be still and silent. A smile can be more effective than muscles; an orgasm can start a chain reaction. A 20-deep circle jerk in the moonlight is a sight to behold.

Our enclosed spaces are so commonly associated with loss: bars close, bathhouses close, nightclubs close, bookstores close. We memorialize them for their raids and riots, fight for our neighborhoods, graffiti their walls in the language of war. But you can't close a natural cruising area. You can mow it down, burn the bushes, send in cops, but it grows back, even if it takes a decade or two. They survive plagues, wars, depressions. Before we had walls and bars, we had only the outdoors to find one another.

Cruising in nature is one of the last truly anonymous places. We still leave clues in sex clubs or bars, open ourselves to judgment, gossip, social media sleuths. There are benefits to anonymity. It allows us to explore our fantasies, what Truman Capote called "building a lie" of our lovers. Here, you can still build that lie, decide how you want to hide or reveal who you really are.

This is not a utopia. It is still beholden to the roles and hierarchies of gender, race, ability, and youth. These can be places of brutal superficiality and privilege. Nature is not always fair or kind, but she's delicate, random, and beautiful.

Cruising the outdoors is nature shaking its own hand.

These tips can apply to all cruising areas, beach dunes, lakes, and temporary spaces like festivals or Queer campouts, but they're tailored toward parks. And while it may not be "classic" cruising, meeting a hookup from the apps outdoors can be an exciting and convenient digital/analog hybrid.

Know the area. How old is the park? Has it ever been raided? Lots of cops? Just being at a park after-hours can be illegal, so scour the internet for any news or reviews to check if sex-seekers frequent the area. Cruising areas don't tend to move, so the old web, like early message boards, are a great resource. The best source is asking an elder about their experiences.

Dress the part. We're here to project our fantasies. Be the trade you want or what you want them to want in you. This is also camouflage. A more neutral archetype may be safer, depending on the area. Play with your desires, but if you aren't familiar with the spot, save the bright colors and big reveal for your underwear.

Ease into it and always trust your gut. Scope it out, see what time feels safer to you. Some folks feel more comfortable in daylight or under the cover of darkness. Share your live location with a friend. If you aren't fully convinced or start to feel uneasy, don't do it. Nobody is rushing you and you got nothin' to prove or lose.

Leave your valuables at home and bring a small bag. Nothing more annoying than having your pants around your ankles trying to get to a bottle of poppers or lube. Keep sex stuff in a backpack or fanny pack. Leave your credit cards, cash, and jewelry at home. If you're going far, stash a $20 bill in your shoe in case you lose your phone and need a cab. Don't carry drugs.

The Museum Technique. Exactly how far do you stand in front of someone when cruising? A rule of thumb is to pretend you're in a museum. Walk around at the same pace as you would in an art exhibit, and use a similar volume. You are either the art or the viewer, so mosey around or stand and wait. Take off your headphones, put your phone away, and pay attention. If you're interested in someone, walk to them and stand at the distance you would from a painting.

Eye contact is the mother tongue. Use gestures and signals like nods, smirks, taps. This silence is as much for safety as for fantasy.

Implied consent in a park. As with a basic street cruise, hold eye contact as you pass. Either of you may tug your crotch or stroke the other's arm to establish consent. Tilt your head toward the direction you'd like to take them. A polite rejection may be a soft shake of the head or simply looking the other way. If someone touches you but you aren't interested, a simple tap-tap on their arm is enough. If everyone is being cool, a verbal "no" is rarely necessary, but don't be afraid to use it.

If others are having sex and you'd like to watch or join, the same rules apply. You'll know if they want company by their location. Have they hidden in the bushes, or are they out in the open putting on a show? You may stand near them, touch yourself, and wait for one of them to touch you. Sex charges the air, so others may form a circle around the show. This is why circle-jerks and orgies are common outdoors.

When you're done engaging with someone, a soft pat on the back or a verbal "thank you" and a smile is enough to say goodbye. Don't feel pressured to small-talk unless it feels right or you'd like to leave with the person. It's not uncommon to make a new friend.

These are spaces for hunters, not predators. If you don't follow implied consent, or if you're rude, you will be expelled one way or another. Don't underestimate how protective others can be of each other. Ask for help if you need it. Leave if there's only one other person and they make you feel weird or unsafe in any way.

Leave no trace. All it takes is one child to pick up a used condom in a park, and before you know it, the bushes are trimmed, or police start to monitor. Avoid littering.

The park doesn't owe you. Nature has no agenda, rent, or liquor sales; it provides what it wants. You might not find what you're looking for, but you may be what someone else needs. If you view nature cruising as a desperate last resort, it will never give you what you seek. If you are patient, empathic, and appreciative, it may show you what no other space can.

Everyone should worship and be worshiped in a garden once in their life.

darkroom

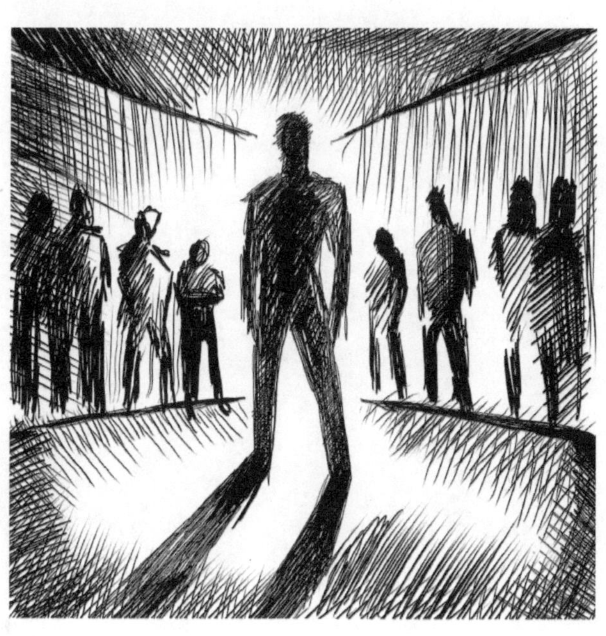

Manhattan, 2011

I was at a Pride party of hipster Queers which had taken over a Hell's Kitchen cabaret. The promoter was a bear DJ / furry porn star named Schwarz Plush. "I turned the green room into a darkroom," he grinned when we came in. My friend and I ran upstairs to check it out.

The furniture was cleared out. The vanity mirrors where drag queens and Broadway wannabees got ready were covered in black tarps. The room could fit about a dozen people, and was lit by a massive blacklight. There was a bathroom with a shower too, in case things got *real* messy. We were thrilled. A darkroom, in *Manhattan*!

The island was once teeming with sex spaces but AIDS, Giuliani, and hyper-gentrification had done a good job of scraping the sexual grunge off the city's nightlife. This was the twilight before PrEP's revolution shoved sex back down the city's throat.

I was three vodka crans in when I picked up a bear couple on the dancefloor—a towering, dark-haired daddy and a cub half his age. "You should let me do terrible things to your boyfriend's ass upstairs," I told the daddy. They looked at one another in that wordless couple negotiation, and daddy nodded.

"I've never been in a darkroom before!" the cub said with wonder, looking around at men in various states of sex. He pressed his chest against the wall, spread his legs like an arrest and promptly pulled his pants down. Daddy put a big hairy hand on my head and pushed it down, making a sweet curly motion on my earlobe. I got on my knees and right as I was about to have dinner, a brutal white light flooded the room. Two queens came out of the bathroom, wiping their noses, leaving the door open. The bathroom light lit the darkroom like a DMV.

The cub looked around like a deer in headlights. In a flash he pulled his pants up, gave daddy a look and bolted. Daddy sighed. "He's Broadway famous." He gave me a consolation kiss. "Maybe later, handsome." Without the shroud of darkness we all came for, the room cleared out.

I was licking my wounds on the dance floor when my friend came down with the same look of blue balls. "That fucking bathroom light keeps emptying out the darkroom," he growled. We ran to Plushy. "I'm sorry, guys. There's no way to turn off the light—the switch is in the club's office, and I don't have access to that," he said, crestfallen. "Trust me, I'm as mad as you are. It's fucking up the vibe!"

"I got an idea..." I whispered.

"Step back and cover your face girl!" My friend grinned and did as I asked. I took the flask from my back pocket. I jumped as high as I could toward the light. It took three tries, but I hit the bulb with the flat side of the flask. It broke off at the neck and exploded against the bathroom wall.

"I've wanted to do that since I saw *Body of Evidence*." We let out a drunken cackle.

It only took the length of Azealia Banks' "212" for the darkroom to fill with bodies. Maybe it was the euphoria of Pride or the rare mix of Hell's Kitchen muscle Gays and hairy Brooklyn Gays, but everyone went completely *feral* and stayed that way until last call.

Later in the night, Plushy came down from the darkroom looking very satisfied. We smiled wide at him. "What did you two do? You know what, I don't wanna know!" He handed us drink tickets.

I never did find that couple again, but by the end of the night, the darkroom rewarded my vandalism with a little otter from the Upper East Side. It was his first time in a darkroom.

A darkroom is a great intro to cruising. It has the easiest learning curve and demands the least effort of all sex spaces. It can also be the most intimidating because the system of implied consent can be difficult to decipher. A darkroom is usually attached to a nightlife space with loud music and little light. There is no talking, almost no eye contact, and consent depends on caressing cues.

A darkroom can be anything. While a bathhouse requires nudity and cleanliness and a park requires vigilance and foliage, a darkroom needs just walls and low light. It can be an alcove at the back of a bar, in a club basement or the bathroom. I've seen darkrooms built out of trash bags and a single red light bulb.

One of my favorite active darkrooms is in one of Manhattan's last divey Gay bars. The bar has relocated three times in 20 years, but its darkroom is still the same. Even the smell remains intact. This darkroom starts off with the light stench of all old bars—mildew, booze, and disinfectant—then it mixes with cologne, Equinox body products, and balls.

Boys arrive pretending they don't want to use the darkroom, but about an hour and a half before last call, it fills up to immobility. Shy boys and looky-loo tourists pack into the tiny space for a frantic free-for-all of groping and sex. At closing time, the boys scramble out before the bar blasts the overhead fluorescents.

Every darkroom has its own rhythm and story arc. The darkrooms in New Orleans' 24-hour bars are gradual and languid, since nobody is in a hurry for the bar to close. In Berlin's fetish bars, sex athletes keep the darkrooms steady, no-nonsense and acrobatic. In Mexico City, Catholicism can hang over the darkrooms in a shy, polite cloud. In San Francisco, darkrooms are at expensive parties with designer drugs and sci-fi lighting. The seasonal summer darkrooms of Fire Island and Provincetown burn with the fever of vacation sex. In Pensacola, the local watering hole hides their darkroom in a backyard foam party.

Darkrooms are everywhere now. In the decade since PrEP defanged HIV, they've flourished. A designated sex space can make parties a little lighter too. Gay men tend to get tense and rude when sex energy has nowhere to go. A darkroom functions as a pressure valve. What unites all darkrooms is how the crowd inside moves in unison. It becomes a jumble of limbs and moans, like a school of fish.

A darkroom isn't a space. It's an *entity*.

San Francisco, 2023

My boyfriend and I were at a disco rager. Disco music never really lost its grip on the city, and neither did the sex values of the 1970s, when darkrooms were native to its Gay bars. The discothèque was in the massive basement of a nightclub on a fentanyl-poisoned street. It was a DJ booth with a dozen disco balls spinning on the low ceilings. LED lights washed the crowd in pinks, blues and crimson. The darkroom was a long corridor that ran parallel to the dancefloor.

We were drunk off extortion-priced whiskey served past the legal hour. My boyfriend held my hand as we walked down the sex hallway (unlike my ex, he enjoyed cruising with me every once in a while). On one wall, men were fucking in slings, blowing each other and jerking off on long benches. On the opposite wall, under red lights, a line of dozens of men waited to be chosen. Every few steps, a drop of perspiration dripped from the ceiling and hit my shoulders.

The open secret of long-term relationships is that once you've seen each other snore, fart, and cry long enough, you don't objectify one another sexually as often. But the dark gives us distance; our bodies once again become beautifully foreign. I can imagine him as a stranger who just wandered in. Amidst all the bodies seeking connection, I always get a burst of appreciation for the one I have when we're in these spaces.

We reached the end of the corridor, the blue lights from the dancefloor contrasted with the deep crimson of the darkroom. My boyfriend was lit out of an *A24* film. His eyes, droopy with Jack and gingers, gazed at me. "Want a blowjob?" His long eyelashes glistened from a very eager disco ball right above us. I nodded. There wasn't much space left, so we parked ourselves at the entrance, breaking the membrane between the darkroom and dancefloor.

As he got on his knees, men walked by, glancing down but maneuvering politely around us. It was perfect, except for one thing. "You can't help it, can you?" My boyfriend rolled his eyes as I got up on a stool to unplug the disco ball.

Put your wallet and phone in your front pocket. Pickpocketing is big business and a big problem in darkrooms. Use a fanny pack or cuff bag. Shove your ID and credit card in your sock, or use a wallet chain. Don't put valuables in the same pocket as poppers or lube—it's too easy to drop a wallet with your pants around your ankles.

Let your eyes adjust. The most obnoxious thing in a darkroom is when you're on your knees, and some blind idiot rushes in and elbows you in the face. If it's pitch black, gently put your hands out very slowly to feel the space, starting at waist level to avoid people giving head. Reach the closest wall and stand still while your eyes adjust. Do NOT shine your fucking phone light. Pre-iPhone, darkroom cruisers would light a joint or cigarette and use the flash from the match to see the room. If your eyes aren't adjusting fast enough, pretend you're checking a text very quickly and use that burst of light to scope the room. And finish your drink before you go in—nobody likes kneeling in spilled beer.

Stay off your phone. This is not the time to send a text, check social media, or browse sex apps. Being on Grindr while cruising is like ordering delivery at a farmer's market—it's pointless and makes you look like a dick.

Move with the darkroom. Is the energy frantic or mellow? What does the space need? More people standing around than on their knees? Lots of bottoms with their asses out? Figure out how you are needed here. A darkroom is about providing as much as taking.

Stand or move *with* the room—it's a living organism. If the crowd is just walking in constant circles or bumping into one another (I call this "the washing machine"), go get a drink and come back when it settles down.

Talk less, come loud! As in most sex spaces, full conversations are frowned upon and should be kept to curt sex negotiations. However, sex noises and orgasms are not only welcome, they foster sex energy. Don't be afraid to let those rip! It lets the room know things are happening and sex begets more sex.

Implied consent in a darkroom. Darkrooms are the least verbal sex spaces and eye contact is nearly impossible, so consent depends on *caressing cues*.

Use expressive and explicit body language to let others know what you're into and what you are not. Lead their hand *exactly* where you want to be touched. To make contact, you may reach out with a firm but polite touch of their crotch or ass, though it is rude to grope without first touching an auxiliary area, like their arm, belt or small of their back. If they walk away, they are not interested. If they stand still, you may continue to explore with your hands. Being a voyeur is acceptable as long as you keep a distance. Some people like to be exhibitionists and others need privacy. Even in a darkroom, manners are important.

Implied consent in a darkroom means you will be touched and may touch, but entering a darkroom is *not* a contract. Implied consent can be rescinded at any time. But if you're in a darkroom without participating, and being rude, you're taking more than you're giving. When in doubt, ask yourself how you would like to be treated. The golden rule is crucial in the dark.

Rejection. In the dark, rejection needs to be unambiguous. If someone touches you in a way you're not feeling, firmly but politely tap-tap them on the arm or hand. Swatting or hitting someone's hand away as your first recourse is against darkroom etiquette. If they don't get the hint, go for a verbal "no thank you." If it's too loud or too dark, grab their hand and place it at their side. Give the benefit of the doubt if it's very dark. Someone may touch you again not realizing it's you. But if they keep touching you, they are breaking implied consent. "I said NO, don't make me tell you again," loud enough usually works. Nobody wants to be the creep.

If you are the one who was rejected and someone taps your hand, take the L and move on. Don't take rejection as a reflection on you. Darkrooms can be overwhelming for some folks, so they may be taking it in or changing their mind.

Sex spaces are self-regulating. There is a lot of testosterone in the air and threats are not tolerated lightly. Repeat violators are eventually exiled by the crowd. If a darkroom isn't "calibrated"– if there's too many newbies or too many fucked-up people – someone violating implied consent may need to be removed by a third party.

In that worst-case scenario, you may need to alert the party promoter first, then the bartender or staff. Be aware that many darkrooms may be operating illegally and the space's owners may not even know about it, so involving any visible authority figure needs to be considered *very* carefully.

Oral. To receive oral, find a place near a wall and

unbuckle your pants. If you have an erection, you may pull it out. If someone is on their knees waiting to give oral, stand in front of them and wait for them to reach and touch you. They may touch your legs and buckle area first to make sure you're into it. A gentle touch of their shoulders, caress of their face or earlobe can be an effective solicitation. If you're feeling shy or unsure, unbuckle your belt but let them unzip you (some folks really love this unwrapping part). To give oral, get on your knees and wait. You may get someone's attention by touching their calf or belt. If the room has some light and you're feeling *real* peckish, you may kneel in the center.

Slings. Some cruising areas will have slings or a sex apparatus like a St. Andrew's Cross. The etiquette is similar to a gym: first come, first served, but don't hog it. If it's free, relax into the sling and take your time to show your goods or jerk off. But if the darkroom is packed, a good rule of thumb is that if you haven't fucked on it after 20 minutes, hop off and let someone else take a ride.

Be gracious. If you listen closely, the most common words in a cruising areas tend to be "thank you." If someone gifts you an orgasm, express gratitude! Even if you'll never see them again—or can't even see them now. Reciprocation is not usually expected, but if someone really worked me out, I give them a big kiss on the cheek or forehead before I leave, or a similar tender gesture that says, "You are a person and not just a hole." Even if being just a hole was the whole point.

If the sex chemistry was especially amazing, bring 'em into the light for a drink, exchange numbers or say thanks on the apps later.

A darkroom is a privilege that takes planning, law bending, participation, and communal discretion. It's a chance to go through a looking glass most people can't. Even if you did not get what you wanted, you should express gratitude to be there, even just to yourself. Where else on earth can we make a friend in the dark?

arcade

Phoenix, 1999

The first time I got cruised was at Castle Megastore, a gigantic porn emporium. It was in a gray, brutalist building near "the gay" Denny's (AKA Jenny's), Phoenix's closest thing at the time to a gayborhood. As soon as I turned 18, I headed to the Castle to buy porn after years of surviving on a single stolen *Playgirl* and pixelated internet photos.

The Castle had no windows but was lit by bright office fluorescents and had sparkling white linoleum floors, shelves of fuzzy handcuffs, and overpriced lingerie. I proudly showed the attendant my ID and dove into the discount bin of $10 four-hour VHS tapes of old Gay porn scenes stitched together.

In the back was an area that sucked the light out of the place. It was some kind of dungeon, behind a maroon theater curtain. Above it was a blood-red neon sign that read "Video Booths," with a smaller, hand-written sign that sold "$5 tokens."

I was curious but that was half my budget. Besides, why would anyone want to watch the porn at the store? I wanted to get in and get out as fast as I could before anybody saw me or my parents' truck.

As I flipped through the videos, I felt someone watching me. I turned around and locked eyes with a man standing outside of the booths. He was older, built, with a baseball cap and cargo shorts. I didn't have Gaydar yet and I was still a virgin. Everyone seemed to judge my Gayness in Phoenix so I figured he was just judging me for looking through the tapes. I paid him no mind, paid for my treasures and bolted.

I felt like such an adult leaving with my loot, even though I was speed-walking, paranoid someone would see me. I couldn't park worth a damn, so my parents' monstrous F-150 was at the end of the lot. Ever since Matthew Shepard was murdered, I looked over my shoulder more. The man was following me.

The walk to the truck was interminable. I turned around again, and we locked eyes. He looked serene yet aggressive. I was confused and scared, freaked out but excited, dizzy with conflicting feelings. When I got in the truck, my body just paused on its own, as if it were buffering. The paralyzing hesitation only lasted a moment, but that was all it took for him to get to my window. I looked straight forward, started the truck, and drove away, half expecting to see him in my rearview mirror, chasing me on foot like the T-1000. But instead, he shrugged and walked back into the store.

Now I understand that my eye contact and that critical pause had been an invitation. How was I supposed to know? Nobody had taught me how to cruise. Guys who did that in movies always died one way or another. I will always regret not cruising the video booths with him and demystifying sex then and there. But I also know it would have been like having a burger after starving on a deserted island: delicious, but more than my body could handle.

New Orleans, 2023

My friend and I were feeling lazy, but it was a Friday night. There was a sex party, but we weren't in the mood for stuffy muscle Gays in Nasty Pig snapbacks and neoprene harnesses.

He got a glint in his eyes. "Adam and Eve?" We'd been talking about hitting the video arcade for months. We jumped in the car and drove half an hour to the outskirts of the city. It was desolate and industrial, the air thick with swamp and oil refineries.

Arcades hide in plain sight, usually in the back of adult shops. Louisiana is dotted with them, stores with names like Adam and Eve, Le Video, and Mr. Binky's. I pass them on road trips, when they're not a turn-on with a stomach full of fast food and car sickness.

Like most porn shops, it was lit by blinding fluorescents. The standard DVD and sex toys lined the cheap shelving. The door to the arcade was toward the back. We paid a very sweet and polite young woman $10. "Theater on the left and booths on the right."

The "theater" was two rooms the size of a very tiny doctor's office, with the same chairs. A flat screen TV mounted on the wall was playing Gay porn. Three older men were transfixed on the display. In the next room, another TV played straight porn while two men jerked off from opposite ends of the row of chairs. One was older and the other was in his mid-30s, his legs spread open, jerking off a giant penis.

Suddenly a booming voice called out my friend's name. It took me a moment to realize it was the guy with the big dick. "What's up man, sit down."

It was so jarring to hear someone be so loud in a sex space. He sounded high as fuck, but even the most tweaked out queen manages to keep it at a library level. I tried to figure out where I'd seen him before, but my Gaydar wasn't picking it up. My friend gave me a shrug then sat down, and they started jerking off together.

I let them be and checked out the next room where the booths were. Judging by how cheap the place looked on the outside, I didn't expect much. I've seen booths that are just three pieces of unpainted plywood and theaters that are one TV in an empty basement.

These booths were nice—spacious, more like a small office cubicle, with thick wooden walls painted white, a solid door with a sturdy handle and lock. The air smelled faintly of Fabuloso, as if it had been cleaned not too long ago, but not too much. A sex space can't be too clean. A mop and bucket were stashed in the corner, and I wondered if the girl at the front had to be the jizzmopper—

and if she kind of liked it.

The cubicles had a generous television mounted on the wall, playing four simultaneous screens of bisexual porn. A small tablet on the opposite wall controlled the porn with endless categories. A lavish, leather executive chair stood proudly in the middle of the booth. Two ample glory holes, wide enough to fit two fists or an ass, were carefully carved out at the side. Someone had spent coins and time mapping this out.

There was nobody to appreciate the space with, so I walked out to the store. It had been transformed into a liminal space, the moat to the castle. I browsed the videos, waiting for my friend to come out or for someone to walk in. The door opened and a younger guy walked in. He was a corn-fed, freckled ginger in a green Adidas tracksuit, bright curly red hair, and a huge bubble butt. In other words, my Kryptonite.

He walked over to the straight porn section,

quickly picking up a DVD and intently reading the back. He didn't look around once—his eyes stayed low, and his brow furrowed. My Gaydar wasn't going off. People move differently in a porn shop. Their joints are stiff, gaze to the ground. They either quietly rush in and out, or they overcompensate, giggling and taking way too long. Sex creates a distortion field.

I stood at the back of the shop and watched him, waiting for him to turn around. Was he here to cruise the arcade? Was he just a straight college student buying lube or condoms? Or a newlywed with a kid at home, just looking for a peaceful place to jerk off?

He walked over to the register, and bought a small box of something, maybe boner pills. He handed the girl cash and mumbled something that made her smile. She handed him his change and motioned toward the back.

"Praise the Gayngels," I thought, as he walked his

thick legs toward the theater. I stood at the entrance, and he gave me a quick glance as he rushed in. Younger guys can have trouble holding eye contact so I didn't let that discourage me.

He walked in quietly and I followed. I watched his face as his eyes adjusted to the dark. What would he think of the three older men sitting down? Was he looking for a daddy? The soft and generous blowjob of a local? Or was he waiting for bayou trade to lift him over their shoulders? A twink to protect for the night? I was neither of those.

I watched the negotiations in his face. The older men were definitely not for him. He walked into the next room, where my friend and his friend sat. "Hey man!" The guy's booming voice again. The young man mustered a soft wave and just stood there, as if he was auditioning for both of them. I didn't know the deal with the loud guy, but I knew my friend was only into tiny twinks. Both guys looked back at the screen and kept jerking off.

The young man looked over at me with more negotiations. He walked to the room with the booths. I followed. The three older men had already made their way over and were standing at the booths, auditioning for him. He was immediately disappointed.

I locked eyes with him and I motioned my head toward the booth. I also added a little shrug that said, "*I'm all the Prince Charming you got, baby.*" In the distortion field, I couldn't tell if that was pitiful or if I should be proud.

I didn't wait for him to respond, I just walked into a booth, sat on the chair and waited. A few minutes later, the boy came in and got on his knees.

It was a toothy, selfish blowjob. I stopped him, flipped him over against the wall, and got my munch on. He jerked off and came quickly. I didn't (not that he cared). Without the post-nut clarity, I thought maybe he was just shy and rushed—maybe we could try this in a bedroom. I asked for his number. He shook his head, baffled, and huffed, "I mean, it was fun but..." Then he bolted.

"Well, I just humiliated myself," I told my friend when I got in the car. He grimaced. "Who was your loud-ass friend?"

"That's Tom. You met him on the street during Mardi Gras."

"Oh my God, yes, with his wife and kid in that little red wagon!"

We burst into hyena cackles and drove away.

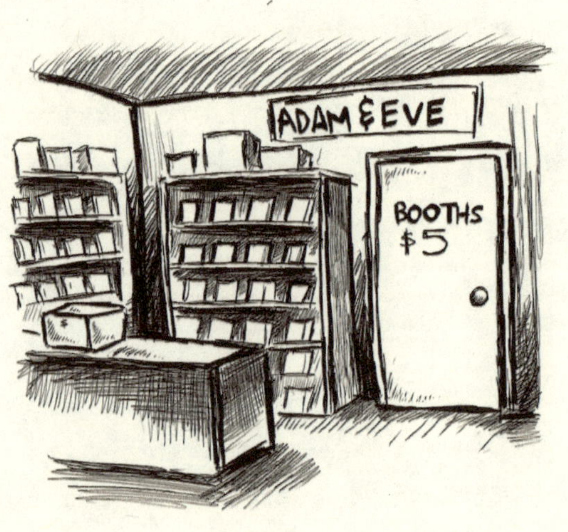
ADAM & EVE
BOOTHS
$5

Arcades are a wild card. The sex spaces of an adult shop are advertised as video booths, adult arcades, mini theaters, private rooms, or peep shows. Every space will offer different amenities and privacy. Leniency for sexual activity varies too. Whether there are locks on the doors usually depends on local laws. Some are strictly jerk-off booths for one, while others are built like sex clubs. There may be tiny booths with a curtain and a single screen, office-sized cubicles with multiple TVs and thousands of digital channels, a screening room with theater seats, or just a basement with one projector and a kitchen chair. Some can be pretty grimey and others are spotless. You can let it be a surprise or do a quick internet search before. Some people love to review these spaces.

There may be an entrance fee charged at the cashier. Or you may purchase tokens to run the booths. Other places don't charge at the front but will use your credit card to unlock the booth and turn on the TVs. Some will have time limits. There is usually huge, clear signage on how to access the area, as the last thing a cashier wants to do is answer the same question all day. The areas are generally toward the back or side of the cashier. Expect to spend $5-15.

Above all, it's a business. You are not going to get back there without forking over some cash. And this is a good thing. Otherwise they become toilets, or places for people to do drugs or take naps. Every space is different, but the one constant is that they're going to take your money before you can get your rocks off. Some arcades are meant to be the McDonald's of cruising: ya get in and out as fast as ya can and it's normal to feel a little gross after.

Post-nut clarity inside a porn shop can be an odd, sleazy feeling. Media has not done these spaces any favors. Porn shops and sex arcades are usually portrayed as places of degradation or violence, used only by desperate, lonely people, peeping toms, and addicts. But they are an important, albeit small, part of the Queer sex ecosystem. Adult arcades may not spark the Queer imagination like other cruising spots—I've seen obituaries for closed bathhouses, never for a closed video booth—but they're a rare public area where the entire Kinsey scale can coexist in a sex space.

The shop is foreplay. Cruising starts here. It's kind of naughty to be in a store that you can get laid in, lean into that. It's okay to browse the porn, get yourself hot and bothered. There is usually no way to tell the vibe in the sex space until you go in. That's half the fun.

People usually shop alone, so a handy way to gauge the action is to count the cars in the parking lot and compare them to the number of people in the store. A ton of cars but no one's shopping? There's probably a party back there. If the sex space is empty, shop while you wait. Don't waste your whole day waiting, though—try another time, like after work hours or on weekends.

Don't waste energy on being embarrassed. Hesitating before you go into the sex space is normal but you're not doing anyone any favors by pacing around, sweating and debating whether or not you're cruising the arcade. The cashier sees hundreds of people and most folks just want to shop and mind their business. As long as you're not a creeping on them, or loudly chatting up strangers, nobody cares that you're in there.

If you can, buy a little something. Pick up some lube or poppers. Using the store for essentials is a good way to establish a connection with the sex space.

Implied consent in an arcade. Arcades require extra thought and caution when it comes to sex and consent. Not all spaces allow sexual activity, not everyone is looking for man-on-man action. If you are caught having sex in a space you shouldn't or not paying for the booths, not all stores are run by a sympathetic Gay person.

How the space is set up will usually tell you if sex is permitted. If the booths have glory holes or if the space is open with no privacy, you can assume sex happens there.

Many folks don't have a place to jerk off in peace. They might be married, in a college dorm or in the military. And if that's your thing, this is a great place to find all three. That demographic may not be acclimated to sex space etiquette so be thoughtful to get an explicit invitation first. There is usually no security guard to help out if you misread someone's cues and things get heated.

However, arcades in known Gay shops and

neighborhoods are usually very lenient and have similar implied consent cues as sex clubs and darkrooms. To establish implied consent, stand around the booths or the hallway. Relax against a wall and wait for eye contact. If that is sustained, send the invitation or wait for it, usually someone tilting their head toward a booth or grabbing their crotch. The rest of the interaction will follow the same consent guidelines as other sex spaces like bathhouses or parks.

Rejection. Don't establish eye contact. Don't approach the glory hole or engage if they do. If someone reaches out to touch you, the universal sign of sex space rejection applies: just tap-tap them on the arm or hand or give a verbal "No thanks." If they are really not getting the hint, just walk out to the store for a minute. If someone makes you feel unsafe, leave.

Glory holes. Throwing neck at a glory hole is both ritual and transaction. That tension is what makes it a Queer icon and a staple of most sex spaces.

If you are in a booth with a glory hole, step inside and wait. If you're in an arcade, turn on the porn. When someone comes into the next booth, give them a few moments to check out the space. If there's a chair and they sit down, they most likely want to suck dick. If they stay standing, they're probably looking for a blow job. If that's unclear, depending on the glory hole, you may be able to establish eye contact.

Lean down and quickly—but deliberately—look into the next booth. This isn't a peep hole; it's a glory hole. It can get creepy if you're just staring, unless they're an exhibitionist, in which case they may jerk off while making eye contact through the hole.

For a more explicit invitation to suck 'em off, put your fingers or hand up to the glory hole. You don't need to be too suggestive or stick your finger and hook it in a come-hither way. It's just to let the person on the other side know that you're open for business. Anyone looking for sex will be very alert of the hole, so it doesn't take much.

To get a blowjob, stand at the glory hole, unbuckle your pants and wait to see if they approach the opening. You can stick your whole erection into it, but that can be either rude or hot depending who's on the other side.

There's the transaction of fluids and flesh, the ritual of worshiping on your knees. But for a long time, a glory hole was the only way that men who had sex with men could let one another know they were in the area. Like little Gay mouse bites. A glory hole is not just ritual and transaction, it's also a beacon.

sex club

San Francisco, 2016

"Ready to go to Dad's?" my best friend whispered at the house party while queens rambled over a mirror. "*I thought you'd never ask,*" I said with a look.

Dad's was our code word for Blow Buddies, the sex club in the SOMA. It was our refuge after the bars closed, when afterparties got stale with powders and trauma dumping.

There was a ritual to arriving at Blow Buddies. The tense small talk in line. Signing the waiver, like a little contract with the devil. The liberation of checking our phones into heavy metal lockboxes. The way our keys clinked in them with a prison-like finality.

We would sneak in a flask or even a six-pack and just sit and gossip in the courtyard while the place filled up. There was ritual to our separation too. The moment when the smell of sex cast its trance and the purpose of our visit bloomed. "There's one for you," we'd say when we spotted trade the other would like. Bars are sets for competition, but here we rooted for each other.

Getting lucky here meant a blowjob worthy of the name. Blow Buddies was all about oral sex, and in the confessional-sized booths, it was the ultimate ritual. Blow Buddies opened in 1988 in the middle of the AIDS crisis, and after bathhouses closed in 1984. Oral was less risky for HIV transmission, and the club built itself around harm reduction ahead of its time.

Blow Buddies was in the industrial South of Market neighborhood, home to dozens of leather bars, most of which closed while Blow Buddies remained standing. It survived through a blessing of zoning. The lot was reserved for commercial use or manufacturing, with a maximum allowable height of 30 feet. This meant no condos or box stores. Blow Buddies felt as eternal as its website, which hadn't been updated since 1997.

The entrance was a thick leather curtain leading to lockers and a clothes check. It was all lit by red bulbs. There was a relaxing room with a vending machine and a random barrel of peanuts. The courtyard was surrounded by booths with saloon doors and gloryholes for al fresco blowjobs. Most of the inside was a labyrinth of booths, black lacquered wood with glory holes carved on all sides. Thick and cold metal chain curtains separated areas. A single sling was parked at the top of metal stairs like an altar. If you climbed the stairs, you could look down at all the booths, like a mouse maze.

The pièce de résistance was the area I dubbed "The Coliseum," a bi-level ring of booths with glory holes at crotch and face level. I could walk into the lower level to a menagerie of dicks sticking out at my face or look down and make eye contact with whoever was sucking me off. It was ingenious.

Blow Buddies serviced all clientele, and I watched the city change here. Older men who avoided eviction or drove from rural towns soon gave way to wide-eyed techie nerds on PrEP, seeking the hedonism they had heard so much about.

The club couldn't survive COVID-19. Their website was finally updated to announce, "The club was created in response to one virus and done in by another." A few local articles reported the closure. Gays who never went mourned the loss and called it "an institution." When I'm in San Francisco, no weekend goes by that my friend and I don't say, "I miss Dad's."

New York, 2011

I could never find the Bijou in the daytime. But after the bars closed, I could locate it like a homing pigeon. It was in the East Village, a plain building with a nondescript door, marked only by the number 82 in gold. Later, the door became covered in graffiti and stickers, making it even harder to find.

I could show up alone or bring trade when neither of us could host. I never tired of the expression on their faces when I opened the door and revealed bright red stairs leading down to a basement—their eyes wide in the golden light as we stepped into an old New York.

Elizabeth Taylor, Marlon Brando, and Humphrey Bogart gazed from posters lining the walls down to the bottom of the stairs, where Nicole Kidman stared at us from a cheeky, giant *Eyes Wide Shut* poster.

A man behind a glass ticket window waited for $10, then pressed a buzzer to unlock the turnstile that led to a heavy door into the club.

At the front was a pool table, lockers, and a bar that had long been abandoned. The Bijou was technically a theater. There was a big projection screen with sturdy movie theater seating. Behind the screen was a corridor of booths the size of closets. Each booth had a tiny bench just wide enough for one person. In the corner to the left of the screen was a darkroom. On any given weekend, the theater would host all of horny New York: I met cab drivers, Orthodox Jews, closeted politicians, drugged-out partiers, blacked-out European tourists, Broadway actors, and people from the Bronx, Brooklyn, Queens, Harlem, and the Upper East Side.

The Bijou began as a speakeasy called The Rainbow Inn around the '20s. From the '50s to the '70s, it became Club 82, one of the most prominent American clubs for "female impersonators." It was opened by the Mafia, like many of our venues back then. The opulent shows were for a mostly straight clientele and tourists, but attendance began to dwindle in the '70s as the East Village became seedier and more dangerous. For a brief time, it was one of NYC's leading clubs for the glam rock scene. Then it fell into disarray, eventually reopening as a porn theater and sex club in the 1990s.

The movies were random: porn, classics, or hyperviolent action films. I got a hand job to *The Fast and the Furious*, was spitroasted to *Vertigo*, and received a blowjob to *The Hurt Locker*. I once brought an entire going-away party to watch a bootleg of *Maleficent*.

The Bijou was where I'd go if I didn't find anything at the Cock, or after going clubbing. After I came, sweaty and hot, I'd head to the exit, which opened onto a little alley. In the summer, rats and roaches scurried; in the winter, that blast of cold air was sobering for my long trip home. There aren't many spots in Manhattan where a broke Queer like me could feel a sense of ownership, but the Bijou was one. It was my private joke in the jaws of the city.

Typical of New York's lack of sentimentality, the Bijou didn't have a grand closing. No press release or social media post. It didn't even have a website.

A sex club has to start in the imagination. A bathhouse follows a formula: a shower, a steam room, maybe a sauna and a hot tub. But there are no rules for what a sex club should be—it can be anything. An empty warehouse with a single couch, a maze of private rooms, or an immersive art installation. A sex club can be a Frankenstein of all cruising spaces: a bathhouse's showers, a darkroom's maze, an adult arcade's porn booths, and an outdoor area. The smallest comforts sing in the fog of sex—a place to sit, a vending machine, a colorful light accent.

I may not recall everyone I've had sex with at a club, but I remember their most thoughtful details: the TVs that played only static in the booths of the Bijou, providing the perfect lighting; the roaring fireplace at 321 Slammer in Fort Lauderdale; the drawer pulls high above the glory holes at Blow Buddies so you could get leverage; the concession stand run by old ladies at the Cine Savoy in Mexico City selling *palomitas*; the replica of a subway car in El Sexto Piso, with a fake conductor's voice and an LED wall that simulated speed; the trough on top of a shipping container that funneled into a piss shower in Berlin's Lab.oratory; the decadent air conditioners and silk curtains in the sex tents at Burning Man. The best clubs should feel like a playground.

Of all the play spaces I've been in, Blow Buddies and the Bijou came to me at a crucial, thrilling stage of my development. During Covid, I was overwhelmed with loss when some of my favorite Queer bars and restaurants closed. I never wept for these two spaces. I took their loss with the same stoic, loaded brevity of their departure. But on late, restless nights, I still feel them like a phantom limb.

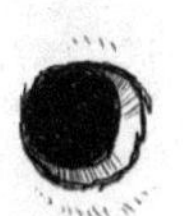

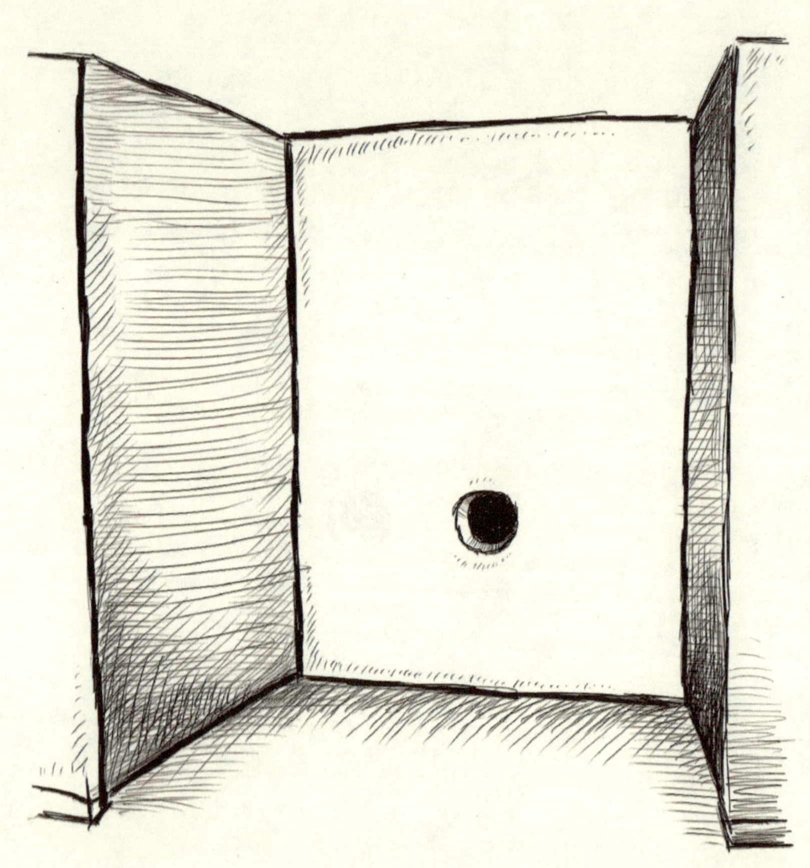

Checking in. Sex clubs may charge a single cover, a membership fee, or both, typically ranging from $20 to $50. You'll get a key or lock for your locker, which may be a separate charge. If there's a clothes check, you usually put your clothes in a bag and may be assigned a number. They may store your ID, phone, and valuables. If drinks are available, you'll most likely pay after. Some clubs are even BYOB and may check your bottle behind a bar. Private rooms or booths are usually first come, first served, but nicer clubs may charge for them. You might strip down to your underwear, so carry your sex gear, like lube, in a small, light bag.

Timing is everything. Try to pick a time where there's action. Unlike a bathhouse, most sex clubs don't prioritize relaxation. Holidays and weekends after the bars close are usually a good bet. Clubs that close early may be more full right after folks leave work or during lunch hour. Check their calendar. Some will have special fetish nights, like pissing or fisting or dress code. Ask friends.

My friend told me to arrive at a sex theater in Mexico City on a Wednesday at 2 PM. It seemed oddly specific, but there was a ten-person line when I got there. Turned out, Wednesdays were half-off and workers from the nearby farmer's market filled the space after they finished working. Word of mouth reveals things the spaces can't post online.

Implied consent in a sex club. Sex clubs fall between a bathhouse and a darkroom in terms of consent. Like a bathhouse, touch is space-specific. Touching someone in common areas, like the entrance or locker room, requires overt or verbal consent. As you move into darker cruising areas, glory holes, and slings, consent shifts to caressing cues, much like in a darkroom. Conversations are fine in common areas, but avoid them in the sex maze, darkrooms, and glory hole booths unless they are for sex negotiations.

Rejection may need to be more explicit in clubs, especially in darker areas. The ol' tap-tap or a "no thanks" that is polite and definitive is enough. Some may have booths or rooms which are similar to a bathhouse. If someone is in a room with their door open, the invitation will be mostly non-verbal. Stand at the doorway for a moment and hold eye contact. Wait for their invitation or rejection. Most people in a sex club will be versed in etiquette and it's easy to pick it up fast.

bar

Provincetown, 2010

The ferry dropped me off into a wet fever dream. The beach town was a '50s Americana fantasy. White picket fences exploded with hydrangeas glowing in the July sun. As I biked to my campsite on the dunes, every pier, candy shop and seafood restaurant was inhabited by big, burly men. The streets were packed with bears. Hairballs rolled at my feet like tumbleweeds.

"Queen, you're about seven days late, it's the end of P-Town Bear Week. They'll be gone by tomorrow, then it's Dyke Week." My friend had stopped cruising the dunes long enough to deliver the tragic news. This was my first time, on a last-minute invite from DJ friends who did not love bears like I did. He placed a consoling hand on my shoulder. "You can still catch the underwear party if you hurry."

I hauled ass back to my tent to throw on a cute pair of undies, then booked it to the last party. I tossed my shorts and shirt at the clothes check twink and ran to the pool area. The party was sparse. The Top 40 circuit remixes couldn't revive the sunburnt, grumpy bears shuffling around dead-eyed in jockstraps and tighty-whities, sipping their drinks and lipsyncing softly to themselves.

A bitter taste was forming in my mouth. The only thing worse than FOMO is being late to the party.

Then he came in. A towering, 300 pound, hairy pork chop of a man. He had a black beard and chocolate brown eyes under teen-idol lashes, with rib bones the size of my femur and a belly in golden ratio to his bubble butt. The Fibonacci sequence in bear form.

He looked around like he'd lost his bike. He wasn't in underwear, just jeans, hugged by a blue-checkered lumberjack shirt, dark chest hair bursting out like the hydrangeas. He looked like Gaston's thicker brother. He walked to the pool and the bears turned like zombies to a gunshot.

He was *fresh*. All around me, the cupcakes had all their frosting fingered off, but this one was still in its shrink wrap. Then, a queasy realization: this was the hottest bear I had *ever* seen. I wanted to run away, pretend I never saw him. The only thing more painful than his unattainability would be his rejection.

At 125 pounds when wet, when you're my size you're *invisible* at a bear party. Most bears would more likely try to order a drink from me than buy me one. But I cut my teeth on the dive bars of San Francisco, trained by fearless elders, drag mothers, and old bears who had survived more than a little rejection. They taught me the art of the bar cruise.

So I chugged my drink and marched my skinny ass over. Even over the tribal beat of Deborah Cox's "Nobody's Sposed to Be Here," I could hear my heart pounding in my chest. I stood far enough from him so I could lock eyes without looking up.

"What's your name?" I asked, staring into his

deep, dark eyes.

"John."

"John, I'm Leo. Where were you before you got here, John?" People like to hear their name.

"I just got off the bus from (a rural town I can't recall now). My first time here or at any bear party. What about you?"

"Well, this is not my first bear event," I smirked, "but it is my first time in P-town. I didn't even know Bear Week was a thing."

"Yeah, I couldn't get the time off work, so I only made it here for this. I have to be on the bus by midnight," he said sadly. "Looks like we're both late to the ball."

A long, shy silence. It was now or never.

Bars are built on little white lies. *I'm not broke.*

I'm not socially anxious. I'm not painfully horny or insecure. I'm not here looking for someone to make me feel pretty. I'm not a nerd pretending to be cool. In a place built on facades, candor can be the sharpest weapon. I don't know what came over me —maybe the tequila, the blue balls, or my friend staring across the bar giving me a thumbs up. I felt an undignified soliloquy of white-hot honesty pour out of me.

"Look John. You are one of the most beautiful men I've ever seen. I know I might not be your type...So I just want you to know...You don't have to look at me now, you don't even have to look at me during, and you sure-as-shit don't have to look at me after. All you'd have to do is close your eyes and let me suck that dick. So take a look around and if by last call, you don't find someone who wants to fuck you as much as I do, you find me."

Before he could decide if he should be insulted, flattered, or intrigued, I patted him on his giant bicep and walked away, like a marine biologist sticking a tracking device on a dolphin.

"He is *so* hot. But he made such a weird face! What did you say to him?" my friend asked.

"Ya don't wanna know," I groaned, embarrassed with myself. I didn't see the dream bear again for the rest of the party.

The pool closed and the event wound down earlier than I expected. I got in the clothes check line, planning how early I'd get here next year. The circus of sloppy bears was doing a balancing act on one leg to put their shorts on. The evening was a fucking flop. My last hope was the Dick Dock, the cruising spot I'd heard a few jokes about.

I put my shorts on, turned to leave, and there he was—an encore apparition, towering over me. He somehow looked even hotter than before.

"Ya know, all these big guys wanna fuck me but all I could think was, 'Where's that little guy?'"

I felt my ears flush and a schoolgirl giggle frog-leaped out of my throat. He laughed and blushed.

There was *no way* the cheap inflatable bed in my tent could survive what I wanted to do to this man. I pictured riding him down a river, like Mowgli and Baloo, leaving everything behind.

"Been to the Dick Dock yet?" he grinned and shook his head.

The town was like a Queer Cape Cod replica at Disneyland. We were lit by strings of lights and the moon as we walked down Commercial Street, teeming with life. Bears who were leaving tomorrow chatted with the lesbians who arrived early. Parents on day trips from Boston walked wearily behind kids feral with sun and sugar. Neither of us said anything; we just looked around, overcome by the town's beauty and our own anticipation. The phallic Pilgrim Monument, modeled after Italian architecture, towered over all of us.

The Dick Dock was underneath a bar on a pier. We walked down the sandy stairs, past circles of bears jerking off and fucking on the beach. We walked away from the crowd and found a private little spot.

"I really want to eat your ass," I blurted.

"I've been traveling all day, I haven't showered," he said politely.

"Trust me, I won't mind a little tang," I grinned. I poured my flask down his hairy crack and ate his salt and my whiskey to the sound of bear whimpers under the dock and tiny waves lapping against tiny boats.

When we finished, he walked me back to my camp, his giant, warm hand wrapped around my slender fingers. Every few blocks, we'd look at one another and grin. Neither of us asked to exchange numbers. Sometimes, perfection requires goodbye.

I faithfully returned to Bear Week for ten years after that, but I never saw him again. I've picked up many men and been rejected by many more. I've had countless wild nights at the Dick Dock and more romantic strolls down Commercial Street. But that was the closest I've come to a fairy tale cruise.

Eye contact is still the mother tongue. Learning to hold eye contact when we cruise is about more than just our eyes—it's about deprogramming our sense of self-worth and safety. Two areas which, let's face it, have been historical challenges for Queers. We learned to avert our gaze as a survival instinct, avoiding other Queer people to not be "found out." It's also a reflection of our insecurities; when we think someone is too hot for us, we dart our eyes away. A bar is a safe place to practice this skill. Learning how to take up space and communicate with one another is one of the reasons we created these venues. Once you can hold your gaze at a bar or club, it becomes easier in all cruising areas.

Don't assume everyone wants to fuck their clone. Many of us will stop ourselves from approaching others who don't match our body. We think muscle guys are not into bears, or a bear might not be into twinks or a twink might not be into daddies. "They'd never be into me." This self-sabotage perpetuates body segregation, one of the most frustrating and limiting aspects of bar culture. When you hit on someone who doesn't look like you, you're breaking those cycles.

When we teach ourselves to *only* have sex with our clones, when we don't experiment with different bodies and archetypes, when we tie our self-worth to only those who make us look good or who our friends think are hot, we get stuck in a feedback loop of diminishing returns. Conquest becomes more important than real pleasure. We lose the ability to discover and evolve our sexual tastes. We view our partners as trophies and our bodies as passports. In the end, we only cheat ourselves. We leave the window open for body dysmorphia or substance abuse to calm our insecurities. We may disguise casual racism and transphobia as a "preference." As we get older, aging adds its own brutal dimension.

The more we expand who we "allow" ourselves to have sexual interactions with, the more centered and confident we may feel. Who we are attracted to is not a reflection of our worth, and we don't always have to fuck a mirror.

Everyone wants to feel pretty. If done with respect, compliments are a great icebreaker. If they are patronizing or fetishizing, things can go south fast.

Clothes are a safe option to compliment ("I love the color of that shirt," "Those are great shoes.") The way they dance, their smile, or even the way they laugh are great too. Those are things we tend to be insecure about.

One must be thoughtful with physical compliments. If the setting is body-forward (such as a pool party or shirtless circuit dancefloor), positive reinforcement about their body can be welcome. "I would kill for your arms" or even a "Damn, that is a beautiful ass." But be aware of racial fetishizing. "I love Black men" or "Do you have an uncut Latin dick, papi?" can diminish you and the other person.

Like so much of cruising, letting someone know you are attracted is not always about reciprocation. Sometimes, it is just a nice thing to do. Like so many gestures in cruising, it's a deposit in your karma bank—you never know what someone is going through. A compliment from a stranger could make their night, whether you get laid or not. Some of my favorite friendships have started with compliments that didn't lead to sex.

Implied consent in a bar. There is no implied consent in a bar space. Unless it's a bar-darkroom hybrid (e.g., a leather bar like The Eagle) keep your hands to yourself. Communicate through eye contact and body language. Only after flirting for a bit and getting some kind of invitation is it okay to have body contact, such as a light stroke of their arm or a caring gesture like moving hair from their eyes.

The greatest pickup line. Starting a conversation with an attractive stranger is nerve-racking. Your mind can go blank or turn you into a rambling idiot. How can small-talk not sound rehearsed or desperate?

A pickup line should not be a yes-or-no question, but should open a conversation. The cliché of "come here often?" is a terrible line. It's one-sided and binary. Some people are shy, and even if they are interested, they might just say "no" and freeze up, leaving you standing around. A pickup line is both a shield and a weapon. It should prevent rejection from getting too awkward for both of you. It should allow you to walk away with some dignity intact.

"***Where were you before you got here*?**" is the perfect pickup line. It always has an answer and a response, no matter how nervous both parties may be. It allows space to gauge interest and read body language. If they say, "nowhere" and turn around, then you know they aren't interested. If they say "dinner with some friends," and start batting their eyelashes, you can ask where they went. Or if they say, "at home, and you?" *Boom*. You're in a conversation. The hard part is over. In a verbal cruise, words are secondary. Courage and attraction are what's really being gauged.

You don't need to seal the deal right away. Let someone know you like them early on, then find them later or let them come to you. This is not about playing hard to get but allowing people to settle into the space. Bars can be overwhelming. Let them hang out with their friends, or, cruel as it may sound, weigh their options. Unlike other cruising spaces, where you cash out immediately after eye contact or invitation, bar cruising can be a long game of catch and release.

The "sidewalk sale." Bar cruising is not over when the bar closes. The peak cruising time is outside of the bar or club, especially with that cutie you locked eyes with or spoke to before.

Embrace "no." Rejection sucks; there's no way around it. When I was learning how to cruise, one of my elders taught me that "The worst thing someone can say is 'no' and that leaves room for someone else's 'yes.'" If you accept that and repeat it yourself like a mantra, you can cruise anyone.

Don't police pleasure. Cruising got a bad rap for a *long* time as we faced the trauma of AIDS and generations of sodomy laws and police brutality. Many people still say cruising is gross or that these appetites are why we're "not accepted" in society. They'll ask why our culture focuses so much on sex with all the struggles and horrors in our world.

Pleasure is not binary. It exists alongside fear, sadness, and politics. That *is* the history of Queer pleasure. We tend to tell one side of our history—of riots and martyrs—but ignore how much sex is a root of that liberation. The folks who judge and police another consenting adult's pleasure are just policing their own. For the past decade, we have experienced a massive paradigm shift through tools unimaginable to our ancestors: PrEP, HIV undetectability, DoxyPEP, vaccines, GPS apps. Our history is full of Queers who lament eras they missed out on. Stop arresting your own development and abolish the cop in your head, beloved. **We are in a sexual revolution—act accordingly.**

Take care of yourself. Cruising, especially if it's anonymous, puts the responsibility of self-care on you. There may not be a way to contact-trace if you get an STI. Take your PrEP, take your HIV meds, wear condoms if that's your harm reduction. Make sure you're getting checked up. Be honest about why you're doing it. Cruising is challenging on a good day. Doing it for validation and not receiving it, especially when you're already feeling down, can be damaging and prolong healing. And alway, always listen to your gut. Cruising should not just add risk to your life, it should add adventure.

Happy hunting!

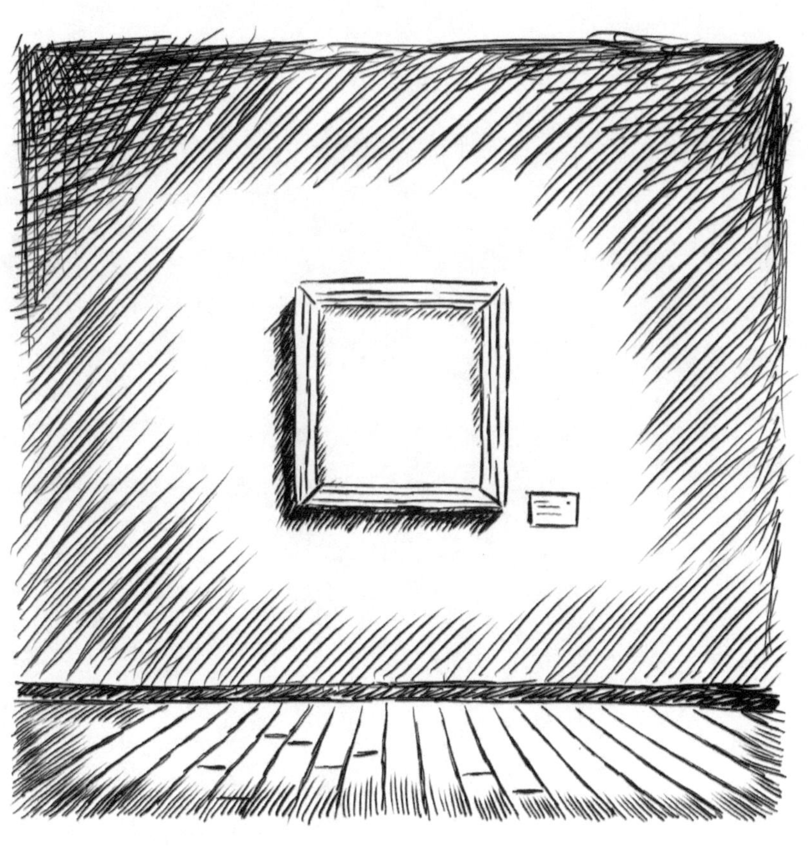

epilogue **(apps)**

San Francisco, 2024

I came to the Bay Area in spring of 2024 to finish this guide. I had a thrilling sex agenda: a bathhouse, three video arcades, a sex club and a speakeasy disco darkroom (which is as fun as it sounds). Instead, I threw my back out moving luggage and spent my trip horizontal on an ice pack. Out of boredom, I loaded hookup apps to my phone. I had a flirtation with *the apps* a decade ago after a breakup, but it was short-lived. They just didn't work for me. But I decided to give them another chance.

Everyone on the apps arrived for a different party. Some were a blurry torso looking for a 2 AM blowjob; others had a dozen portraits and essays for their dream man. Some wanted naked photos, others strictly forbade it. A tap (or a woof or a growl) was either the equivalent of a wave or a marriage contract. There was no way to gauge interest—whether someone was just bored and horny, looking for a little connection to jerk off, or really wanted to meet up. I was ghosted mid-chat or blocked for arbitrary reasons. And never in my years of cruising had strangers virtue-signaled their politics so loudly. "No racists. No Zionists. No Republicans. No Liberals. No Trans. No, No, No…"

I spent so much time scrolling, chatting, tapping, sharing photos, and waiting. Communication was instant or chats were over the span of days. After all these years there seemed to be no common etiquette.

I was shocked at how pay-for-play they had become. Features which used to be free were behind paywalls. I could only access a handful of profiles and photos. There were incessant pop-up ads for anal-brightening soaps and in-app purchases for "boosts" to increase my profile's ranking. If I wanted to be anonymous, I had to pay for "stealth browsing." And that was for a single app. As usual, we had segregated ourselves. There were separate apps: for muscle Gays, bears, scruffy hipsters, folks of color, and the fetish community.

Unlocking one app cost the equivalent of a shift at a minimum wage job. I wondered how this built-in classism contributed to their homogeny. The top of my grids were often the same well-to-do cis Gay men, most often white. As these companies answer to shareholders and roll out new features like AI "boyfriends," the price will increase, leaving more outside their paywall.

When did cruising become a paid utility?

Sure, capitalism has always been part of our sex spaces. Gay bars and their darkrooms were never free. Adjusted for inflation, a bathhouse in the 1970s cost the same as an unlocked app. But these are community spaces that include friends, dancing, maybe even a meal. At their best, they can feel like a family reunion.

The apps have been gamified into a dopamine slot machine. Now I get why so many friends say "I deleted my Grindr" in the same tone as "I deleted my coke dealer's number." Like a coke problem, the apps manage to be both addictive and boring.

The apps can sell anonymity but not privacy. I found myself hyper-aware of what I said or what chats and photos could be screenshot and shared with others. But the main invasion of privacy I worried about was from the apps themselves. The largest companies have been in high-profile lawsuits over selling our sensitive data, like HIV status, to advertisers. They've admitted to training their AI bots on our private messages. Every day, people fall prey to blackmail and financial scams from the same kind of chatbots these apps will market as AI boyfriends.

It feels like all the things that give harmony to cruising—manners, anonymity, privacy—are crashing against capitalism. Digital cruising seems to be in disagreement with itself.

Analog cruising spaces are based on agreement: we are all here for the same reason, following the same rules of consent. They are not democratic, and certainly not utopian, but they exist outside of algorithmic conflict and surveillance. I've never seen a political or racist argument break out in a cruising space. There's no way to catfish one another in person. We can put on a costume, but there's a difference between catfishing and playing pretend. We call these "play spaces" for a reason.

Apps can be very useful, but they're just one tool in a huge arsenal. They serve communities which may not have Queer spaces. They help folks with disabilities, anxiety, and autism. Trans folks, for whom analog cruising can still feel unwelcoming or unsafe, can discuss their gender journey up front. Apps can help disclose HIV status and break stigma, and they are invaluable for disseminating information and contact tracing in a public health emergency like Mpox. New apps which are map-only are a convenient analog and digital hybrid.

But have we used these apps as a crutch to not address our community's issues in the outside world? To not program our spaces to be more welcoming of all bodies? What is the future of an app-only sex diet? If I log into them in another ten years, will I be greeted by synthetic lovers and have to pay for real ones? If my data has been mined, how will I know if the cute boy who chats me up—who happened to guess my favorite movie—wasn't assisted by an AI wingman, knowing exactly what to say? How will I know what part of his photo was enhanced by AI? How will I know if they're even human?

I don't fault us for embracing the apps. Apps aren't killing our bars or sex spaces—miseducation is. You have to learn implied consent or eye contact in person. None of us grew up with mainstream media that celebrated our sexual appetites. People have done such a miserable job of valuing Queer culture and sex. Why *wouldn't* we let machines raise us?

When my back finally healed, I made it to the speakeasy disco darkroom. I took a driverless car to the offices of a non-profit, not expecting much for a Tuesday. Instead, I was greeted by hundreds of men in their underwear. I checked my clothes and found a corner to watch the show. A guy ate out his boyfriend's ass at the bar as a photographer took polaroids for a pretty penis contest. A bear in nerdy glasses was servicing the crowd with a giant dick while a group ran a train on a svelte twink. My friend tenderly kissed a boy with top scars. Queens vogued to a remix of ABBA's "Dancing Queen" under a disco ball shaped like a pig. The scene could have been out of a '70s photograph. The power of analog cruising is its timelessness.

There was no way to replicate this online. The dopamine of swiping and the Pavlovian bells of our phones had been replaced by anticipation and pheromones. Here was only the unforgiving, thrilling present. We couldn't take photos, but we could be visions. So many died creating, protecting and enjoying these spaces, through wars and plagues and financial ruin. Prince Charming may not always show, but when we cruise face-to-face, we honor heaven.

I cheered on the performances for a while. Then I got up to play my part.

Leo Herrera is a writer, activist and filmmaker. A first-generation Mexican immigrant from the small border town of Ascension, Chihuahua. His work focuses on the Queer and migrant experience. His films and writings explore how LGBTQ culture intersects with technology, politics, public health and sex. His sci-fi film *FATHERS* imagined the world if AIDS never existed and was the subject of the 2018 Emmy-winning documentary *Behind the Lens*. His 2007 film *My Name Is Harvey Milk* documented the suit Harvey was assassinated in. He has helmed outreach campaigns to raise awareness for HIV criminalization, Mpox and blood equality, against the FDA's restrictions on blood donations by Gay men. His psychedelic film pieces have been a staple of Queer nightlife for two decades. His work always aims to inform younger generations about our history while simultaneously paying homage to it. A closet comedian, Herrera has also created multiple satirical personas online raking in millions of plays. He resides in New Orleans, with roots in San Francisco, New York and Berlin. He's a lover of jazz, park cruising, grills and run-on sentences.

www.ingramcontent.com/pod-product-compliance
Lightning Source LLC
LaVergne TN
LVHW090610110826
845146LV00001B/335

* 9 7 9 8 9 8 9 5 4 1 8 5 0 *